Quantum Ghosts

poems by

Julia Ponder

Finishing Line Press
Georgetown, Kentucky

Quantum Ghosts

Copyright © 2023 by Julia Ponder
ISBN 979-8-88838-344-5 First Edition
All rights reserved under International and Pan-American Copyright Conventions. No part of this book may be reproduced in any manner whatsoever without written permission from the publisher, except in the case of brief quotations embodied in critical articles and reviews.

Publisher: Leah Huete de Maines
Editor: Christen Kincaid
Cover Art: Arielle Ponder
        @pondering_art_and_things
Author Photo: Julia Ponder
Cover Design: Elizabeth Maines McCleavy

Order online: www.finishinglinepress.com
        also available on amazon.com

Author inquiries and mail orders:
Finishing Line Press
P. O. Box 1626
Georgetown, Kentucky 40324
U. S. A.

Table of Contents

Quantum Ghosts 1

New Year 2

The Universe 3

Green 4

Dear Driver #1 7

Noon 8

Pink Dress 9

Back to the old house: A sonnet 10

Blue Jean 11

At Social Services 12

Welcome Home 13

Dear Driver #2 14

Etymology of "before" 15

Lady Poet 16

The Burning of the Apple Orchard 17

Disembodied Voice 18

Dear Driver #3 19

Naptime Elegy 20

Doppelganger 21

Poem for the Hairdresser 22

Dear Driver #4 23

Poem while watching television 24

Dinner on a Tuesday 25

Bibliography 26

Behind Walmart 27

Albrecht Durer & His Subjects 28

Advice from Yesterday 31

For Kamala After Her Death 32

Post-Covid Poem I 33
Dear Driver #5 34
Proceed 35
The Event Horizon, or How far we've traveled since then 36
Tidying up 37
Verbicide of Mother 38
Post-Covid Poem II 39
La Brea Tar Pits 40
February 41
Shadows: a ghazal of past selves 42
The Mountain's Love Song 43
Vows 44
Old Growth 45
Winter Prayers 46

Special Thanks to my husband, Alex, and my sister, Arielle. Without you, these words would mean nothing. Also, thank you to my mother, who recited poetry for us even when we didn't want to hear it.

Quantum Ghosts

    I
Electrons behave like waves,
and probability decides.
You interpret the wave equation
as randomness,
as shuffling and dealing cards.

    II
An empty field,
then the crashing and
breaking of distant branches.
Birds suffering through the
clouds. Snow was heavy last
night, weighing it all down.

    III
I'm scraping ice from asphalt
when I notice three apples
hanging on the bottom branch of a tree
in a long row of barrenness,
still red, still swollen, waiting.

    IV
Electrons will be in multiple
states at one time.
A moment requires a witness to
convert light signals into images.
You are dead and alive until
someone takes a chance to see
many worlds, many cats,
many tarot packs,
collapsing into
a pool of minutes spilling on the
floor—
Your greatest moment.
Your greatest defeat.

New Year

The new year beckons like
a bruised bone,
moldy green under the skin.
It is a slow cracking open,
brittle but hidden in the sheath of this body.
Each mistake of the year,
each hurt throbs
like a careless echo
sent into the inner caves of memory,
setting off some distant crash.
You press into the spot with your
thumb, hidden inside your pant leg.
You feel the new year there,
a thunder of your fading reflection
in the warming pain.

The Universe

is billions of cells
frantically moving this way
and that

is sewage, plasma,
and bacteria being wiped
clean with a brown paper towel

is rough and
raw on your nose

is vulnerable to the slightest
cough

is that big spoon in the sky
or maybe the little spoon

the universe

becomes these unwashed hands
poking and prodding bulging
empty flesh in the mirror

becomes naked and crying

becomes ultramarine when you sing with
me in the car

becomes
rancid

the universe

begins embracing the expanse

begins finding itself again
the universe
shyly hides underneath the sink
beside the bleach, behind the garbage can

Green

I

There is an old oak
that reaches up beyond
my window into the sky.
I watch as leaves burst
and filter the light that
trickles in
to match its leaves.
I marvel at its size.

II

Everything is green.
Even the old beige Toyota that
sits at the end of the driveway
begins to collect debris and soon
patches of moss invade and cover
the rusting steel hood.

III

I am small.
The shade of the oak tree
creates shapes on my hands.
On summer days, I collect
leaves, stones, and twigs
from around the base. I build a house
for a caterpillar, small like me
in this endless yard
crawling with life.

IV

When my mother is feeling well
we plant sage, cosmos,
Zinnias, and sunflowers.

"Pollinators," she tells me,
singing Crosby Stills & Nash.

    V

My father squats low,
a cigarette hanging out of
his grinning mouth.
My sister and I watch
as he half buries beer cans
along rows of green beans
and corn.
"For the slugs," he says.
My mother giggles.

    VI

Along the white siding
of the house,
facing the east,
grows English Ivy.
Green slips to cover everything
eventually.
The neighbors wage
a war against it on
their lake beaches
across the street.

    VII

Summer is always best,
living becomes effortless.
Even as I grow older,
I still fall asleep in the
grass, using my book
or journal to hide my
face from the sun.

VIII

I slip into these worlds
from my dreams
a million years away;
on Google Earth images,
milkweed and rogue saplings
crowd the ever-shrinking
yard.

IX

My sister paints oil on canvas,
dark swirling trees surrounding
shimmering water; leaves,
triangles of green and a patchwork of
chain link fence that keeps it all in and us out.

X

Not pictured on Google Earth:
Yellow caution tape that says,
"Dangerous, hazard, enter
at own risk."
I take comfort in knowing
the green will slip in
eventually.

Dear Driver #1

Dear Driver,

I am sorry I ran that stop sign. You pressed firmly into your horn five times, and I sped away shamefully. If you could peer closely at me in the driver's seat, you would see that I was going there and back again. It happens a lot in the car, or when I'm walking on the sidewalk, or when I'm teaching a class, and suddenly I stare off into space because something a twelve-year-old said made me quantum leap back in time. It's not important. I know I shouldn't be bridging the space-time continuum while driving, walking, or teaching plot lines. Shouldn't have my hands holding tight to a swing twenty years ago or feet deep in wet grass five years past. Memory is a safety hazard, always leaping about inconveniently. But I'm sure you know that already.

Noon

Your mother's Audubon clock
is an array of colorful wings
and flattened plastic beaks
pressed into the wall.

Pure magic, it
hoots and squawks

indicating the hour,
indicating
the destruction of
our in-between places.

That clock has outlived
so many.

Even in the darkest of times,
it continues to look on the bright side
while waking the world with a cuckoo.

The talons of the hawk,
the burning eyes of a great horned owl,
and blackest blue of raven feathers

are free in sound for an instant.
Soaring and diving and perching on the
linoleum countertop.
Free in their cries to tell us
that it is 2 am and time for bed.
6 pm and dinner.

Until the batteries die
and long exhales warble through the morning,
distorting the chirp of the chickadee.

Pray for the minutes lost
standing in front of the refrigerator as it hums,
no bird left to break you from your thoughts.

Pink Dress

I'm tearing holes in my flesh
waiting in the café for a drink
by the corner window and
gnawing, tearing, biting, and
ripping at the skin of my fingers
because of a pretty stranger in
a pink taffeta dress.

I want so badly to be like her;
I want to walk around in her
body and discard mine like old
underwear.

The giggles from the counter carry—
I am curled into my book and smell like mildew.

I go to speak, but
my voice spills over into silence.
fish-guts on a pebbled shore.
I gather them back up again,
wondering how everyone goes
about the world so easily.

Back to the old house: A sonnet

Soot does not stick to hands like the feel of
hard work and beauty on fingertips,
which charcoal leaves. Smile, she's done, and you
can see love in the highlight on his bottom lip.

Soot does not sit, not like the subject
whose body breathes. Instead, it forces, binds,
chooses only shadow for you. Do not expect
to ever escape the smell of smoke. In my

mind I can taste it, the sour tang of kerosene.
What the poor lack in central heat, they make
up for in bloody noses and loss of speech.
Hands would tremble; we were not taught to pray.

I should have taught her not to shake, waiting
in the dead of winter for the pipes to break.

Blue Jean

For two years, I've carried your
records in the trunk of my car.

Today, I brought them into
the house for the first time.

On top, a David Bowie
vinyl, plastic wrapper

just slightly peeled back. Now,
a new imagining of your

last day: starting to open
the vinyl featuring 'Blue Jean,'
then giving up.

At Social Services

Remain calm—
we cannot be held responsible
for what happens to you.

We are not in the business of dirty faces
or untidy remarks.

Please remain calm—
fulfill the correct
information for the deceased.

Please remain calm while
we process your request.

We will need both signatures—
His name and your name in print.

Please remain calm and
take a number. Others are waiting.

—your fingerprints and
proof of residency.

Please remain calm
while we process your request.

Take another number to
receive the remains.

Welcome Home

If ever there was
a raccoon in my heart
to bring me back,

it died when you died,
picking through the garbage.

Claws scrap against the inside, torn plastic between your
teeth, choking on bits of bones, and spitting out apple cores,

scuttering up the porch to find the house
more human than we left it, boarded up with longing,
heavy with the weight of all it carried.

I peer into the droopy eyes of the now jaundiced windowpanes.
I am looking for you.

If ever there was
a raccoon to bring me back again,

it died when you died,
staggering through the yard at noon,
digging through rat shit in the corners and in the sink.

Sometimes houses are more human.

Drowsy little beast, tearing at Padlocks, orange paper,
      rifling through the mail left on the mat
         that says, *"Welcome home."*

I never thought you were more human
than after you died.
Now I, too, raccoon hearted, starve on old postcards,
longing for a decent meal.

Dear Driver #2

But, Driver, if you could see, peer through your windshield and mine, see behind my eyes drifting off cloudily into space, you would understand. You would see me looking at my father in a mothball funeral home, laid out on a medical table and dressed in the requested black paisley shirt, black pants, and black cowboy boots he asked for in his suicide note. You would see the watermarks from the leaky ceiling and smell the antiseptic. You would wonder if things might be different if he'd known he would still look dead despite his favorite outfit; maybe then he'd have changed his mind.

Etymology of "before"

Isn't it strange that I can touch myself
while reading Shakespeare or the bible,

notice imprints of chickadee feet in fresh snow
while the dog takes a shit by the fence,

feel the quiet of the orchard in bloom on my skin,
feel the movement of the highway behind it,

vibrating and kicking up asphalt and dirt while
dew glistens so still on wet pink petals.

On my porch, rush hour honks, and a vibrating
road starts waves on the surface of my coffee,

and a missile killed seven children last night,
as they sat readying supper, how do we go on?

Lady Poet

Putting my hand in Schrodinger's
box, I try again to revise the sound
of claws on cardboard.

Bound up in my garage is a raccoon,
not a cat, scratching at the opening
of the famous box as poison gas
does or does not permeate its lungs.

How many more years will be dedicated
to fingernails sticky with bile
and raccoon hair? The sink becomes
a massacre of universes, but I am never

clean, nor do I ever know if the poor
thing lived, only that I am filthy.
Above in a pane of toothpaste-stained glass,
I can just barely make out that the one I look
for is back from the dead.
Lady poets are always writing about mirrors,
but when I look up in the mirror,
I see your reflection, Dad—

combing your hair and scowling, burdened
by age and trying to blur the lines
of your cheeks while scrubbing
desperately at my pores.

The Burning of the Apple Orchard

This morning begins with a molting of limbs.
Today, the ceremonial burning of the apple orchard starts
in a pyre at the end of the road. Each tree is wrenched
from the dirt and dragged to a growing cascade
of branches and ember; Fuji, McIntosh, and Golden Delicious,
have all lost their definition as the inferno
grows, and the sun flees over the horizon.

       It is a purge of past selves, worthy and unworthy,
diseased, pest-ridden, and healthy too.
       Even miles away, the embers beckon
as they dispel, inviting as they caution.

Ash falls like some secret message landing in your gnarled
hands. Already, the neighboring orchards
have started to redden and blossom. Do they take notice
of the scorched earth beside them?

Disembodied Voice

I am reckless
        non-existent   a wreck

destroyed   a heap

how quickly the conversation ends

spoken   forced (never ends)
                              endless questions
how quickly?

like water through the hands.

Dear Driver #3

In the rearview mirror, I see him. The body is rubbery and cold, unmoving despite my warm hands rubbing and touching and holding and pouring over his stiffness. Driver, or should I say, a friend now, I'll spare you the tears and the oh Gods and the turning away because you will experience them someday too, and it's enough to live it once to know. In his stiff, cigarette yellow fingers, we put an unopened Budweiser (glass, because it is a formal occasion) and a picture of us, a gift from Christmas past. Then it is time. He is wheeled away on a squeaky cart to be wrapped in a cotton shroud, all we can afford. If you are the responsible one, you will get the final, smelly wrangle of shitty clothes in an orange plastic shopping bag. I am the responsible one.

Naptime Elegy

These hands have become ancient bedtime
stories slipping on the dewy rim of a glass.

I am waking
up to your ghost again; it waits at the end of my
nap, pleading for me to
avenge you with self-mutilated

thoughts. A haunt from
purgatory like some King Hamlet.

I am so thirsty—
The water I need is close by;
cold fills the spaces of my tired

mouth like a creek
flowing between rocks, lifting pebbles
of memory, taking me with them,
ending at the bottom of a lake.

I'm almost awake, too soft and water-logged
to seek revenge on you—you traitor to self, to god—
traitor to us. We can't meet like this anymore.

I can't see you,
can't pretend to share a beer,
have a father-daughter dance,
can't dream you play on the beach with my unborn
children. I can't.

I make tiny movements, slowly sitting up
but my mind remains
stuck in that boggy half-place
looking to pull you from the peat with me, unable
to watch your legacy decay in those dreams.

Doppelganger

In the misty darkness,
I imagine another me
quite identical
but with more grit.
She cuts the air like
warm butter with her athletic frame
as she splits from me.

But she's a seamstress,
she sews the air right up again
walking into a dense
fog.

Water droplets stick
to her eyelashes.

We split again,
a thousand more hands and eyes and mouths
parting the sky,
reaching for something that
was never there.

Then the fog recedes gently like
some old poet man's hair.
I am alone.

Poem for the Hairdresser

I tell my hairdresser that I've never been able to stop writing them. There are thousands still lurking in the dark of my organs, like pickpockets in a foreign city waiting to take more from me, knowing nothing else. She nods in agreement; for her, every passing cloud is some hurt that floats away with each new line. The tiled floor is filled to the brim with Mommy and Daddy poems, trimmed away with the dead ends. I meet her eyes in the mirror, vulnerable and wrapped in black like a plump raven. In silence, we recite our verses through the mirror. We are pouring them out together like beer cans in the sink; we are watching our words swirl down the drain, the noxious, hungover fumes still lingering in the air. She returns to snipping away my dead ends. I ask her what she thinks of bringing more light back in.

Dear Driver #4

I am the responsible one, but you might disagree because I have interrupted traffic for the sake of a poem. But Driver, I am, so I oversee the arrangements, getting to know Bill, the mortician, and his sons. As he stands to the side in his suit, I wish he was my father, even though I met him two days ago. He saw us on a Sunday. Father's Day. The universe giving a big F U C K Y O U. Unlike the universe or Dad, Bill wouldn't do this to us. He's hardworking. He listens, tells me I am strong, and he's certainly not the type to squat in an old apartment or hang himself in a closet. Bill's funeral home is a family business, even if it smells like mothballs and there are water marks along the edges of the ceiling. My ears are filled with fluid, and snot is gathering on my upper lip. I wish a lot of people were my father.

Poem while watching television

On the coffee table:
mustard
upside down
left out after midnight
plastic cheese wrapper

uncollected sandy remains
a chunk of soot
an old seed
a book

languid listening
of solicited laughter
ha ha ha ha
goes the live audience
after hours
after sex
after the stakeout
after shots ring out

we examine
the dust on the
bygone collections of
old aches and new
sores in yellowing 1940s negatives
we develop it
for the others
but there are orphan prints
left in the darkroom

I was born into
the old way of thinking
chastised for in-betweenness
memories beer bottle mute

observing that a paper plate
can be a vehicle for food
and also a canvas

Dinner on a Tuesday

The second layer of skin, which I have
peeled clean off with my gap teeth,
is still an orange tinge of turmeric.

On Tuesdays, these swollen
knuckled hands poke and prod
in spices. Then, with rough conviction,
try not to sprinkle any meanness into supper.

Yet sometimes, they are ginger
with their longing. Other times, heavy-handed
with the enthusiasm that grips burnt paprika.

In the end, the meal should always sing.
It should call out to the brass of a Hughes
moon and bury its rounded sides within itself.

There, its lunar bliss tenderly pushes through
and lights up the darkness of your mouth.

Bibliography

Post-it note tears,
sunglass dust,
milky rims of whiskey cups;

I struggle to put my finger on it,
because so much depends

on the snow that settles on
a black mailbox with a standing red flag.

Behind Walmart

My corduroy jacket sports a bite-sized
hole chewed by a reckless collie. In the
still useful pocket, I dip my hand in the
remnants of perfectly
sliced hotdog pieces meant to keep her
from barking at passing strangers on the street.

Tonight, on our long walk along route six and
behind Walmart, we rarely see anyone.
Reality here hinges on the fluorescent lights
that scare away the dog star and the rats
and lurking crooked men.

You can't see the stars
when the lights go out; you can't
see the cave drawings on the back of
dumpsters, nor hear the hum of the cars from
the road, fading—it is as if you've fallen
headfirst into the river Lethe,

abandoned by memory
and the way home.

Albrecht Durer & His Subjects

After his master prints

I

Melancholia (1514)

"What is beautiful? I
do not know."

The altar smells like tomatoes this morning,
and she is stuck striking a pose,
a slouchy pout like a cold fish,

while Durer places magic squares, glitter,
Freemason gadgets, and a tube of toothpaste
around her for a still life.

There is also a baby (not hers) smelling
of seaweed. She's not paid enough
for this. But what is she if he, a great

artist, is unable to capture the elegance
she swears by. Who is she without the
roman columns framing her face and

echoes of history falling off the shelves?
The thought grows till it is strangled by
an answer her spirit won't touch:

everything.

II

Knight, Death, and the Devil (1513)

In the gorge, three move through
the bend, slow like winter sap.
                Notice how the
crowded landscape

of day's end pushes all life
to blind action in search of home.
A knight dressed in rusted armor

and dented helm clutches his fist
tight around old blessings written
on thin paper, certain of the two

who watch him, for it is the killing
season beneath the red elms, a time
when shadows change to match

our sin and threaten to pull us
beneath the darkness. Even the once-
loyal dog

abandons its master—
A sort of common weariness descends.
We have heard this story and

lived it. Lost without beginning
or end, you and I wander, always toward
the possibility of redemption,

just beyond the peripheral on a path we
did not take because the woods betrayed
our tired eyes.

Once we missed our chance, but this time
must be different. It will be this time. It
will be this time. This time.

In the gorge, three move through the bend,
steady like winter sap
thawing gray at the beginning of spring.

III

St. Jerome in His Study (1514)

We were so sure
that ours was the right way—that a

(songs of glorious atoms)

heaven could be born from men's visions;
these thoughts and more made me sink into my
chair and pound my heart with comets till
my soul bleeds.

(so long ago)

In that meteor shower, I knew perfection in
mistake: all beauty comes from error. Yet,
centuries alone I stared into the mixing pulp,
looking deeper to answer the beg,
the cry, of endless characters in stone.

(were drowned in love)

Advice from Yesterday

~~Covid~~ **kill**~~ed her husband. Now it's taking~~ **the only** ~~home her kids have left.~~
~~U.N report warns of grim climate~~ **future** ~~unless~~ **humans** ~~act swiftly.~~
~~'Goldilocks virus': Delta~~ **defeat**~~s all variant~~ **viruses** ~~as scientists race to understand its tricks.~~
~~Thousands flee Greek island Evia~~ **by boat as horror-movie** ~~wildfires~~ **rage**.
~~Trump's coup~~ **attempt** ~~grows even more worrisome as new details emerge.~~
~~Former Cuomo executive assistant describes~~ **escalating** ~~misconduct that was certainly not~~ **consensual.**
~~Pace of Taliban advance quickens as~~ **military overrun** ~~three major cities in a single day.~~
~~Dixie~~ **fire mushrooms into** ~~second largest wildfire in~~ **California** ~~history.~~
~~Obama at 60:~~ **Feet on the dance floor, eyes on the future.**

For Kamala, After Her Death

he by the river contemplates his existence as the verses flow in currents, but not one line was spared for empty Kamala.

he by the river falls asleep to its lulling sounds, and when he dreams, he dreams of Gupta, never of cold Kamala.

he by the river admits that all things and beings are nothing to him, even pregnant Kamala.

he by the river experiences a concealing bliss; could he not invite Kamala?

he by the river meets Kamala—what luck! But she is bitten by a snake, and there is nothing to do for Kamala.

he spares no time to worry about the coincidences of bad luck with women and snakes, but I do, and so does dead Kamala.

he by the river is a sham and knows it, their teenage son too, for their egotism killed exquisite Kamala.

Post-Covid Poem I

Snow gone,
the salted earth now
reveals itself.

Nothing will grow where
we made a path for the oilman.

Yes, the first snowdrops have bloomed,
and hyacinths are coming up. All
foliage says, *get your shit in order.*

But I never know what's most important, and
I still can't smell lavender, dog paws, sweat,
or roasting chicken.

Where we salted the ground
no grass will grow;

should we start the vegetable
garden again? Because it is almost time to sow.

Dear Driver #5

We have already put in the shroud those things which we think he'll need most. But when, underneath the hot, eager sun of late June, the mortician and his adult children start to lower the body, I throw in my copy of *The Hobbit*. He placed it in my hands one summer because we shared a love of imagination, the wild arena of escape, and the deep friendship of father and daughter. And I think he might need it going there and maybe back again.

Proceed

Ideas should
be like
liquid in a cloudy glass saucer,
spilling over the edge of

as you carry it down five flights
of precarious winding stairs,
droplets of new words falling
on wet paper
ginger lips, spicy ochre
staining the floor
which is all of you at once.

Explore life by
entering into a bath with your ideas;
let them soak until they wrinkle,

splashes rippling over the porcelain
onto the floor, seeping in.
Forgive your ideas for inviting
mold in without permission,

for your creativity should sustain
you while at the same time it
threatens disaster.

Never let ideas sit too long to
become old stains on a Persian rug,
producing an embarrassing odor to remind you
of what you've forgotten.

Best advice,
add ideas to a soup with carrots, onion, and celery.
Then your ideas will turn into promises.
Drink these promises on a walk,
leisurely or lost among bramble on unmarked terrain.

The Event Horizon, or How far we've traveled since then

The distance from the non-existent center,
where no light can escape,
is the place where our first memories
dance beyond our eyes,
always present but unviewable.
We were there once—

A heaven people talk about
scotch-taped into
our mothers' photo albums:
a pre-light soggy warmness,
being held
in a favorite lawn chair
underneath grandma's lilac bush.
For me, it's all still darkness.

Today, I tried to remember
while snow-coated trees
hushed and whispered, making
the earth sleepy.

In their branches
there are not enough dreams
to complement all the tight spaces.

Today, I thought about how
I hurt you and
how you never make any mistakes.
How suction
cupped to placenta
we'd never say such things to one another.

How once we may
have been perfect.

The mailman pulls up in his truck.
He's wearing jeans and sneakers in the powdery drifts.

Tidying up

My bare feet are dangling over the
edge of the lawn chair, damp with dew
and tingling, when I notice

the swallows are talkative
this morning,
flying between my maple tree
and the orchard.

Alex laments that he's
let the grass grow too long,
and today will be the day he tidies
it up.

He was taught by his father
the importance of a trimmed
lawn, squared, green, uniform.

I mourn the tiny white blooms
who have sprouted in his negligence,
the wild purple salvia, yellow suns
of dandelion head, and the
tenacious mustard brush,

which will soon be sheared
by the spinning blades of his John Deere.

Each bird knows better than I, knows
that despite our best efforts that
the wild will creep in again.

Verbicide of Mother

    his   lover   moth
                                  or

damn it   tender
                          error
Never
                                                      once
                        thought   break

                        debt   bruise
            cut   she
                        sever
                                                    letter
                                      loved

Post-Covid Poem II

Calculated sun specks
move the traffic in my mind
from yellow nail beds. My
neurons try to catch a thought like

fuzzy teeth clamping down on a bit,
enamel on metal, twisting off the
top of a too-tight jar.
Eyes find reason—
The mind
follows to admire
a rusted coffee can
peeking through the dirt.

I dig it up, curious
of its insides.

La Brea Tar Pits

All highways here border on the 7th layer of hell—
Just note the tar bubbling up on the sidewalk
next to where a nice lady in leopard leotards

lies to sunbathe beside a fire hydrant,
her nipple peeking out of her frayed top
as she snores, and L.A. foot traffic never slows.

The pits are deeper than they look, covered
with browning leaves and surrounded by the
yellowing grass of draught. Archeologists

pull a thousand dire wolf skulls from the black,
predators too lazy to hunt themselves who got
stuck trying to chew on half-dead

camels knee-deep in goo. A family
of four is using a stick to try and poke at the
ancient grave. While across the street, a couple

dressed up for brunch waits in line next to
a homeless encampment, planning a visit
to the nearest modern art museum a block away.

Wandering from death trap to death trap,
trying to glimpse some truth from 20,000
years ago, my father-in-law speaks quietly,

"Do you think the cavemen saved each other?"
Someone says no; there is another yes. Eventually,
we decide it would depend on the caveman.

February

Moon, like a chipped pearl
loosed from a string of sisters,
half caressing the sky suspended
in the azure of a clear day,

you depress me. Why are you laughing?
Damn snow is packed in three feet with the
Swells. It blinds me with a whiteness
that does not forgive, and you laugh.

Against the sky, the trees are as black as
midnight. My shadow, long and
desperate, reaches out to them but
never quite gets close enough.

Moon, like a chipped pearl
torn from around my neck,
I envy your listlessness caught
lounging in the sky, apathetic.

Shadows: a ghazal of past selves

I have spilled my shadow, and it is captured
by some faraway stranger who holds it captive;

true, no one can exist on this earth
without a shadow, for we are our own captives;

I have traveled to find mine again, yet
excavating the closet, I have become captured

pouring over old manuscripts and wrinkled sweaters;
I have fallen in past words; I have become captive

to moth-eaten remembrance; I have traveled to the yard
where wormy mud pies and decadent hyacinths capture

me, and I have become part smell of the ground, part sun
escaping the arms of the endless greedy trees captivated

by the growing darkness around stems and sticks
by the lines left on my skin, for I have become a captive

to all the comings and goings; I have become
lost in all these fine sounds and misty textures; I am captured

then in the stillness in the mirror. Shadow
I have found you in the rounded edges of a pupil, caught

without warning dancing in the reflection to find
we are smiling, both of us willing captives.

The Mountain's Love Song

The Milky Way hangs low this night—
Breathing deep, pressed against the granite,
you and I reach up our callous fingertips
to touch Big Ursa, Virgo, Andromeda,
and as ornaments do, they begin to chime.

All across the valley, the soft sound
can be heard. Back to Jackson,
where the engines remain unmoved. It
echoes to Conway and beyond that still.

Even the mountains stay
silent to hear it, quieting the whispers
of the millions of pebbles that rest
along their backs. And scolding the bases,
where the old stones lay refusing to break,
ancient and unforgiving.

Vows

Our past territories
were lands left behind
with a cadence of urgency.

You move your hands
over my body and so
much has changed

since they began. I will tell
you how to complete
this terraforming:

seafoam clouds
wet dirt, starling
air, high altitudes.

You tell me
a thing about you
no one knows.

Then, I reach back
into my topography
and find some edge

to meet yours, some cliff of
longing that is the final
piece. Our secrets intertwine in

a mossy knoll of rock, a fragile
ecosystem that only
we can travel to, barefooted.

Old Growth

Steals into you
with a rush of dirty earth and vine,
beginning behind your eyes in
tickling warmth spread mellow as the evening.

Among the silence, branches sing in gusts,
and with your mouth the sound
is delivered to me.
Would you speak my name in these leaves?

Winter Prayers

This will not be the last

congregation of sparrows
to gather in the empty winter orchard

and comb it for left behind skins and stems;
each picks and plucks

between the muddy aisles of apple trees
scanning the scripture of dirt for

secret thawed places hidden in snow
where their answered prayers lie.

This will not be the last
gust of wind that sends them off again
in search of warmer places and higher things.

Acknowledgments

Grateful acknowledgments to the following literary journals where some of the poems in this book have been published:

An earlier version of the "Dear Driver" series first appeared in *The Sonder Review*

"Winter Prayers" and "New Year" both appeared in *The Dillydoun Review*

"Vows" and "The Burning of the Apple Orchard" debuted in *The Shawangunk Review*

"Back to the Old House," "St. Jerome in His Study," and "The Mountains Love Song" first appeared in *The Stonesthrow Review*

"Dinner On A Tuesday" first appeared in *THAT magazine*

"Etymology of Before" debuted in *Cape Rock*

"Green" debuted with *The Hudson Valley Writer's Guild*

"Quantum Ghosts" and "Lady Poet" first appeared in Turn 3 of *oxford public philosophy*

* * *

Julia Ponder is a poet, author, and teacher living in the Hudson Valley region of New York. Her poetry has appeared in national and local literary journals. Her work exists in the in-between places that we often forget about, somewhere where the pastoral and the autobiographical meet. Late afternoons staring into space, that moment you realized you changed and soon forgot, or the love that tingles in your toes which carries you through the day. Those places—magical and heartbreaking—are where these poems come from.

www.ingramcontent.com/pod-product-compliance
Lightning Source LLC
Chambersburg PA
CBHW020343170426
43200CB00006B/485